The minimum could be defined
as the perfection that an artefact achieves
when it is no longer possible
to improve it by subtraction.

John Pawson

Ballet Shoes, Carmel, California, 1998

ARTIST'S CHOICE

THE PHOTOGRAPHS OF

Rod Dresser

Limited Editions Press

This book is dedicated to Maggi, my inspiration and my love.
None of this would have been possible without her.

List of Photographs

1. Ballet Shoes, Carmel, California, 1998
2. Granite Steps, Carmelite Monastery, California, 1982
3. White Rose, Carmel, California, 1998
4. Building Facade, Bodie, California, 1988
5. Power Tower, Highway 46, California, 1985
6. Dancing Lady, San Francisco, California, 1988
7. Sensual Dunes, Death Valley National Monument, California, 1985
8. Door, Mission Dolores, San Francisco, California, 1987
9. Shadow, Corrugated Siding, Ryolite, Nevada, 1999
10. Sorrel, San Francisco, California, 1989
11. Black Dunes, Death Valley National Monument, California, 1984
12. Calla Lilies II, Pebble Beach, California, 1994
13. Torn Curtain, Window, near Mono Lake, California, 1992
14. Union Pacific, Ryolite, Nevada, 1999
15. Window and Reflection, Ryolite, Nevada, 1999
16. White Dunes, Death Valley National Monument, California, 1985
17. Church Window, Bridge Haven, California, 1989
18. Sorrel II, San Francisco, California, 1989
19. Abstract Dune II, Death Valley National Monument, California, 1992
20. Leaves in Pond, Carmel Mission, Carmel, California, 1981
21. Black Dancer's Legs, San Francisco, California, 1988
22. Death Valley, Assemblage, Death Valley National Monument, 1997
23. Aspens at Dusk, Lundy Canyon, California, 1998

The Simplicity of Things As They Are

Few if any artistic expressions spring forth from a vacuum—few ideas well forth without the seeds of logic. We are often inspired by our thoughts, but perceptions are centered upon our experiences, our emotions and, for the fortunate few, the desire of creation.

Creative experience is the sum of many parts. One critical element is the taking of risks which range from a radically different vision to the embrace of direct aesthetic connections. Risks can be a reaction to—or affirmation of—artistic heritage. To deny influence is at least to acknowledge the importance of the past.

Rod Dresser has formed a style that absorbs and interprets photography with roots in a wide, fertile field of artistic expression. He does not separate himself from the heritage of master photographers who preceded him in a fascination with the nobility of landscape and the sensuality of form. Rod has taken their inspirations, analyzed them, and refined their qualities in a highly personal, honest and sensitive way.

Rod acknowledges the influences of photographs by Ansel Adams, for whom he worked. Ansel was himself motivated by the creativity of Edward Weston, and encouraged by the spirit of Alfred Stieglitz. Rod's interests in the purity of imagery have resulted from his own interpretation of what these masters offer to those caught up in the passion of visual expression through the lens.

In the following pages Rod speaks about his photographs with a spare eloquence. He shows clearly his specific interests in, attractions to, and motivations for reducing a subject to its inherent elegance of form. While some artists aspire to contrive, Rod seeks the noble simplicity of things as they are. And though many of his images are strikingly minimal, their mood is raptly conveyed. Windows speak softly, callas proclaim, sand dunes whisper, and human figures reveal nuances subtly framed.

Most of us live such complicated lives. We rarely take proper time to muse upon the delicacies of the world around us. Rod Dresser offers these photographs as a respite to contemplate the simplicity and elegance of things we might miss completely or otherwise ignore. The power of photography informs, instructs and persuades. We must thank artists like Alfred, Edward, Ansel and Rod for their generosity in sharing with us their visions.

Dale W. Stulz
April 1999

Dale W. Stulz has been involved in fine art photography in various capacities for twenty-five years. He founded the Photography Department at Christie's New York in 1978 and is currently an appraiser and consultant based in Los Angeles.

Granite Steps, Carmelite Monastery,
California, 1982
(detail)

Photograph 2

I was attracted to this image because of the texture and graphic nature of the steps. The shadow of the railing gave a sense of scale and made a rather abstract subject more recognizable. Steps have always held a fascination for me—where does this lead? When I showed Ansel my portfolio in 1983, this was the photograph he found most agreeable.

Granite Steps

White Rose,
Carmel, California, 1998
(detail)

Photograph 3

This is a studio photograph taken with a single box light suspended above the rose. The petals are delicate, tactile, and full of life. I'm sure there is nothing more pure and beautiful than a partially opened rose. Although the subject matter is extremely simple, I hope it conveys to the viewer both my passion for nature and for photography.

White Rose

Building Facade,
Bodie, California, 1988
(detail)

Photograph 4

Bodie, California, is a very unusual place. It is located in high desert, and because of the lack of humidity, structures there have survived the years with remarkable grace. The metal siding on this building has a lovely, dark patina rather than a corroded surface. I was struck with the bleakness of the facade and the simple arrangement of the door and window. The mysterious nature of the scene further persuaded me to make this image. Who had lived there? What lies behind the door and window now? Photographs that ask questions, in addition to providing a provocative vision, are the most engaging for me.

Building Facade

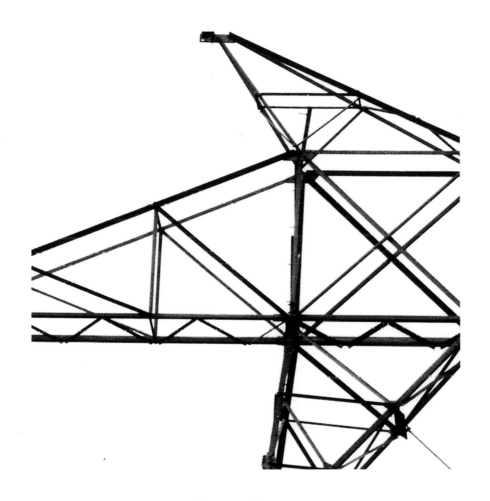

Power Tower,
Highway 46, California, 1985
(detail)

Photograph 5

The power transmission towers throughout California appeal to me because of their very graphic nature. Among man's creations, I think bridges, power transmission towers, and other bare structural elements are artistically pleasing because of their visual qualities. The catenary of the transmission lines and tiny towers in the foreground add to the interest and bold nature of this photograph.

Power Tower

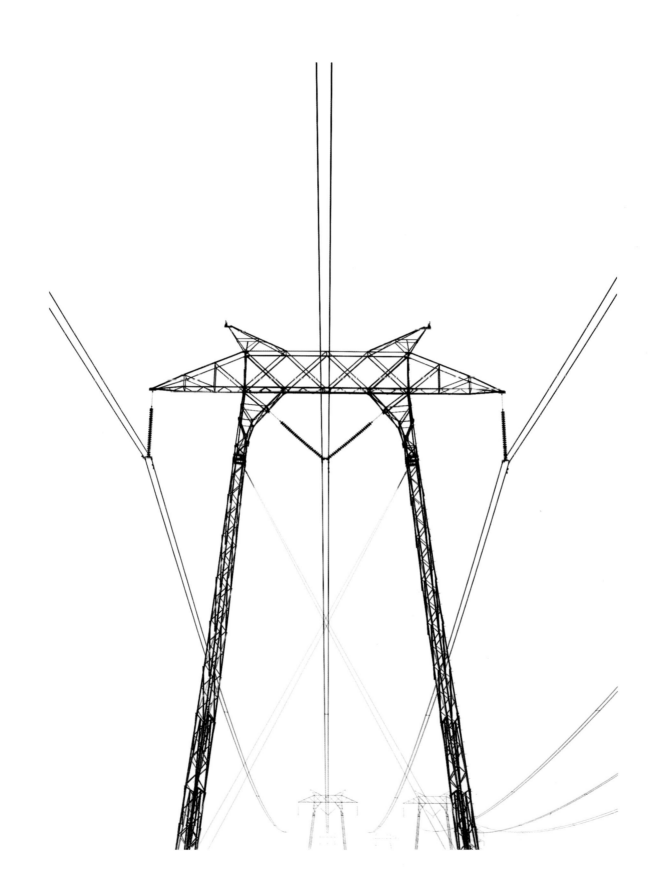

Dancing Lady,
San Francisco, California, 1988
(detail)

Photograph 6

I hired this model for figure studies. After several hours of work, I felt somewhat frustrated because no composition really excited me. The model mentioned that she was a dancer, so I handed her a piece of sateen cloth that I'd acquired at a local fabric store. I asked her to wrap the fabric around her, and to dance back and forth in front of the camera. The only illumination was a large, soft box light off to the right hand side of the photograph. I took four rolls of 120 film as the model danced and wound and unwound the cloth. Of forty or fifty exposures I made, this is the only one that pleases me. I have cropped out the head because I was interested in the light reflected off the sateen molded around the model's body.

Dancing Lady

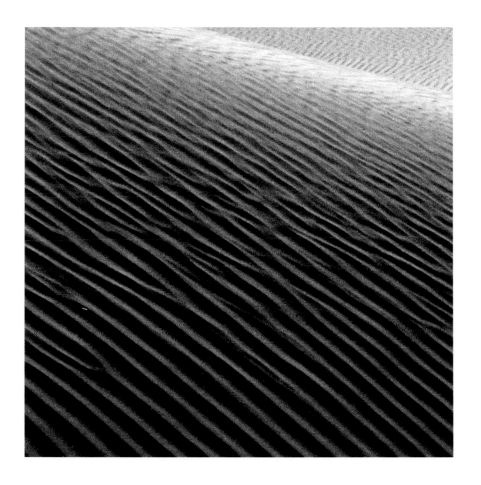

Sensual Dunes,
Death Valley National Monument, California, 1985
(detail)

Photograph 7

Door, Mission Dolores,
San Francisco, California, 1987
(detail)

Photograph 8

In general, I use either a medium or large format camera for most of my personal work. Occasionally I feel frustrated and uninspired, and one of the ways I've found to get over these feelings is to take out a 35mm camera without a tripod, using very high-speed film. Shooting more film, the subject matter and my compulsiveness are opened up. The high speed film permits me to use small apertures for good depth of field, as well as relatively high shutter speeds so hand-holding doesn't inhibit my work. This photograph was taken at midday in a San Francisco mission. I was able to frame the scene carefully, and I'm pleased by the scale of the film and the way it reproduced. The result is a small piece of a larger building, but the door and light on the wall behind it came together for me as a very effective photograph.

Door, Mission Dolores

Shadow, Corrugated Siding,
Ryolite, Nevada, 1999
(detail)

Photograph 9

Ryolite was a silver mining operation that was abandoned in the 1930s. Because it is in the high desert with low humidity, the buildings are pretty much intact. This structure was a service station. The way the light played on the corrugation, and the shadows from the eaves, seemed to me a remarkable composition. I'm not so much interested in taking photographs that are readily identifiable as I am in making images that convey a mood.

Shadow, Corrugated Siding

Sorrel,
San Francisco, California, 1989
(detail)

Photograph 10

Sorrel was a young lady I met in San Francisco. She had an exquisite body and was very comfortable with herself, thus making her an ideal model for my figure studies. I always illuminated her with one soft box light, and over many sessions she would move slightly this way or that, with the light playing upon her nude form. This study reflects the influence of Drtikol, a great Czech photographer who did pictorial photographs of the nude.

Sorrel

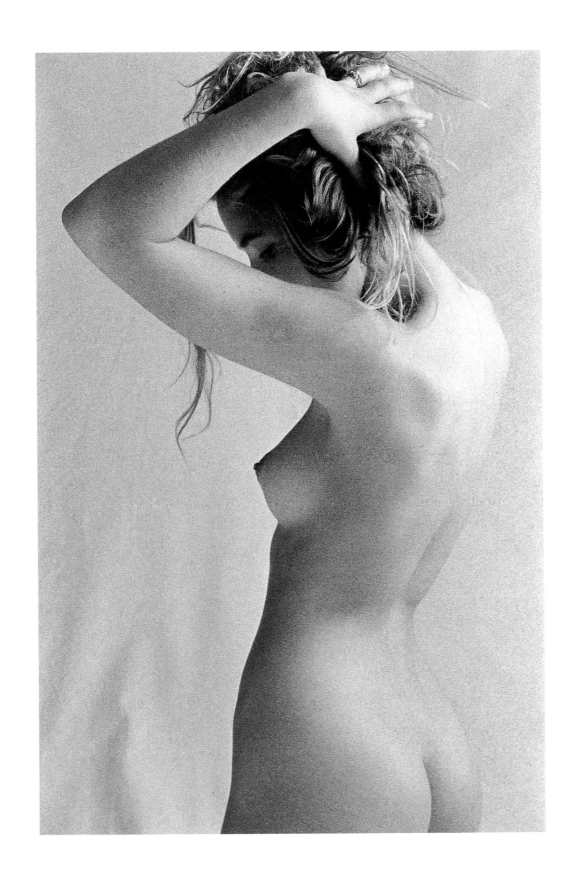

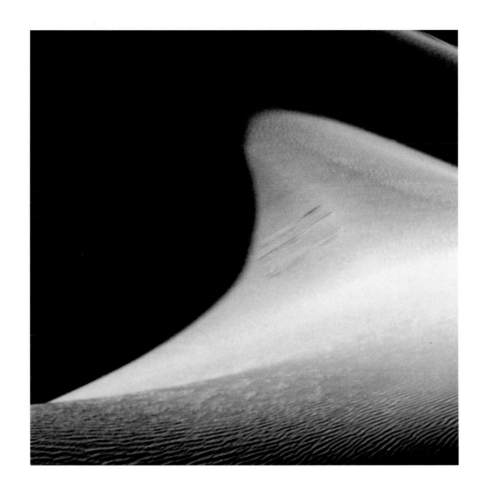

Black Dunes,
Death Valley National Monument, California, 1984
(detail)

Photograph 11

This photograph was made in early morning before the sun filled all shadows with light. I was facing southeast, using a long lens. The layers of light and of the sand dunes attracted me, as well as the near-sunrise deep shadows in the dune crevasses.

The preceding double-page *Sensual Dunes* (Photograph 7) is one of my favorite dune photographs. The forms depicted are very sensual and have many times been compared to a female human body. All of my Death Valley work has been done with a medium format Hasselblad, so I could quickly change lenses and shoot a quantity of film during the short forty to fifty minutes permitted by the changing sunlight.

Black Dunes

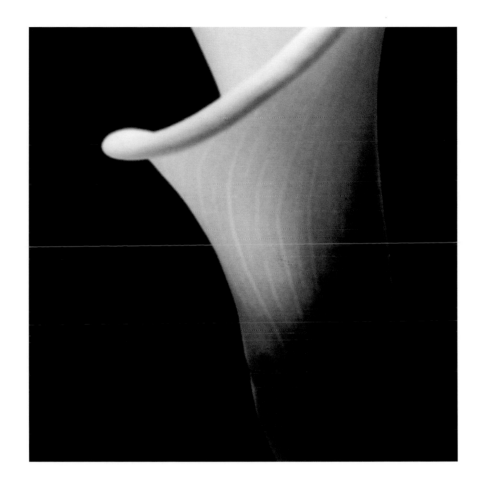

Calla Lilies II,
Pebble Beach, California, 1994
(detail)

Photograph 12

This studio still life was illuminated from almost directly above with a soft box light. Calla lilies are a black and white photographer's dream as subject matter. The pure textured white, the sensual form and the simplicity of lilies makes an exquisite subject. I grow these flowers in my own garden and watch them as they bloom, picking them when I think they will photograph well. I've learned to photograph in the studio in order to keep my skills honed when I couldn't be out in the landscape for one reason or another. I now work a great deal in the studio, as I find its immediacy very rewarding.

Calla Lilies II

Torn Curtain, Window,
near Mono Lake, California, 1992
(detail)

Photograph 13

This photograph was taken in an abandoned cattle ranch north of Mono Lake in the Eastern Sierra. I would say the ranch had been vacant for about forty years but was still in remarkably good condition. Walking into a small room, which I think was a bedroom, I saw light coming through a window and reflecting off a torn curtain tacked to the wall behind it. The play of light and the haunting nature of this abandoned room were compelling.

Torn Curtain, Window

Union Pacific,
Ryolite, Nevada, 1999
(detail)

Photograph 14

In this image are both whimsy and respect. The whimsy part is the existence of a caboose, *Union Pacific 3303,* sitting out in the middle of desert. There are no railroad tracks leading up to or away from the car, nor does the car have wheels. There is, however, a railroad traffic sign about fifty yards away. My respect is for how well the car is constructed. After sitting at this location for perhaps fifty years, and discolored by many winters, it is still intact. The metal parts are not rusted away but have a lovely patina. Perhaps the caboose was an office for someone involved in the Ryolite silver mining operation. Today, it stands as a monument to endurance.

Union Pacific

Window and Reflection,
Ryolite, Nevada, 1999
(detail)

Photograph 15

Here is another photograph from Ryolite: an abandoned building with light coming through a window with broken glass, reflected against a wall at the right side. I got as close as I could—with a medium format camera on a tripod—so as to include no additional subject matter. The viewer is invited to make his own conclusions about the yin and yang effect of the image's two light shapes.

Window and Reflection

White Dunes,
Death Valley National Monument, California, 1985
(detail)

Photograph 16

Church Window,
Bridge Haven, California, 1989
(detail)

Photograph 17

All over northern and central California are small churches that use ship-lap siding. They are always whitewashed or painted a sparkling white. Whenever I see one, I can't resist stopping and looking at doors and windows. The simplicity of this window with its semicircular top, sparkling white siding and mullions made it a compelling subject. I purposely exposed the photograph to make the windowpanes black—my interest was the graphic nature of the window, the panes and siding. Again, my minimalist nature surfaced.

Church Window

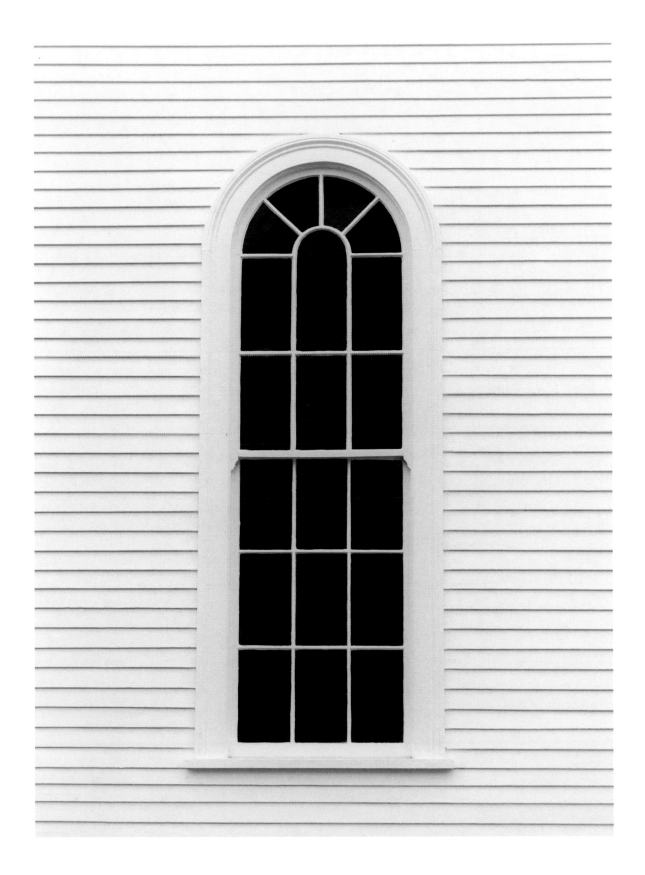

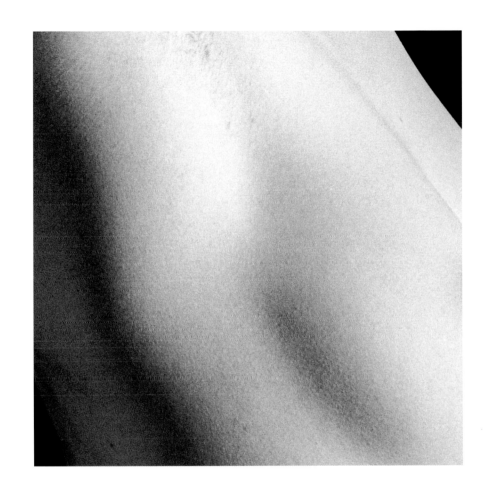

Sorrel II,
San Francisco, California, 1989
(detail)

Photograph 18

This photograph was taken in my studio with a 35mm camera and high speed film in natural (window) light. The impressionist painter and photographer, Degas, has been a strong influence and inspiration for me. His series of women bathing are truly sensitive and beautiful paintings. In my view this photograph is similarly sensual and elegant at the same time. I disdain figure photography that is purposefully provocative, and I do not think *Sorrel II* is such an image.

Sorrel II

Abstract Dune II,
Death Valley National Monument, California, 1992
(detail)

Photograph 19

This is one of a series of Death Valley dune photographs taken over many years. I was particularly attracted by the texture of the dunes and the ways that light and shadow played upon them. Here the dune's ridge delicately etched itself on the sand. The dark shadow made a wonderful abstract form that completed the picture.

In contrast, the preceding double-page *White Dunes* (Photograph 16) is from a purposely overexposed negative. When I looked through my viewfinder, the dunes looked like whipped cream that had been stirred with a big wooden spoon—thus I exposed so there would be nothing but high values on the print. I hope other photographers will become convinced they need not have black or white in an image, but can use grays, highlights and shadows from any part of the spectrum.

Abstract Dune II

Leaves In Pond,
Carmel Mission, Carmel, California, 1981
(detail)

Photograph 20

This is a very early photograph of mine, but a pivotal one. I didn't print it for several years after taking the picture, but was pleased when I did. From my early work, this image is one I didn't consider derivative of Weston or Adams, my photographic heroes. What I discovered and liked was the simplicity and detail. By this time I'd become aware my photographs were too busy, that I should be concentrating on subjects that were simplistic, graphic, abstract, and conveying a feeling of texture and touch.

Leaves in Pond

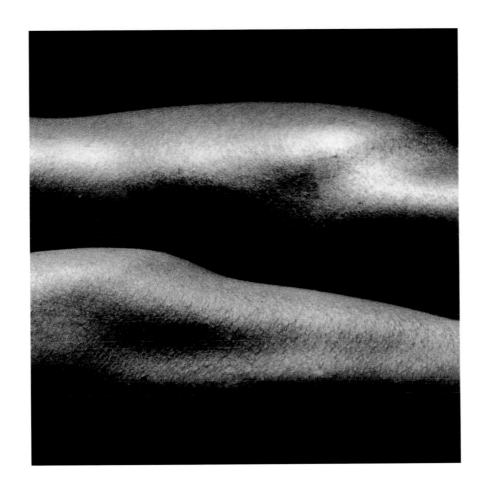

Black Dancer's Legs,
San Francisco, California, 1988
(detail)

Photograph 21

The model for this photograph was a very beautiful black woman who had trained for the ballet over many years. She did not succeed at a professional level, but was an aerobics instructor at the time I photographed her. With the directional light from a single unit above, I was able to portray the strength and beauty of her legs. Their sensual, curving forms brought to mind the sand dunes I had witnessed so often during dawns at Death Valley.

The grace, athleticism and beauty of ballet dancers have always intrigued me. This book's frontispiece, a studio photograph of ballet shoes, tells of dances yet to come. Isolated by my chosen framing, the satin luster and each stitch and ribbon are exquisitely defined. In appearance and construction, these shoes clearly result from years of development and history. They speak to me of the timeless dedication that dancers bring to their art.

Black Dancer's Legs

These photographs are the result of annual trips to Death Valley National Monument for the past ten years. They were taken in an area about seven miles long and two and a half miles wide, near an oasis called Stovepipe Wells. Black and white photography in Death Valley is challenging for two reasons: the landscape is monochromatic, and during most daylight hours there is very little contrast. One must photograph at sunrise or sunset when the light is rich and the sun is near the horizon, creating long shadows. I prefer dawn— hiking into the dunes before sunrise allows me to set up my camera at a location that hopefully will be productive. When the sun creates the funereal mountains, deep shadows accentuate sensual and abstract forms. To witness the sunrise is an artistic and spiritual experience. Circulating winds cause the dunes to change every day, and each sunrise produces new images. My assemblage interpretation conveys the majesty and serenity of dunes and surrounding mountains, as well as intimate details of rippled texture. Sharing with others these delicate and temporal forms, shapes and relationships is very gratifying.

Death Valley, Assemblage,
Death Valley National Monument, 1997

Photograph 22

Aspens at Dusk,
Lundy Canyon, California, 1998
(detail)

Photograph 23

Lundy Canyon is a small road just north of Lee Vining, off Highway 395 in the eastern Sierra. About two miles from 395, before reaching Lundy Lake, are several groves of lovely aspen trees. I have photographed them many times—almost always after sunset. The eastern sky becomes a wonderful light source, softly illuminating the aspen trunks. The trees seem to glow in their own light. I usually use a long lens so I can isolate portions of the trunks, not having the image too busy with extraneous foliage. This image has an Oriental quality in terms of its simplicity and abstractness. As with most of my photographs, I find less is more—the minimalist's clarion call.

Aspens at Dusk